TIPS, HIN~~TS~~, ~~...~~, CHEATS AND WALKTHROUGH

Disclaimer

The author has tried to be an authentic source of the information provided in this report. However, the author does not oppose the additional information available over the internet in an updated form. The objective of providing different tips and tricks to the players of Dragon City is to help them play their best. The information included in this book cannot be compared with the guidelines provided with other apps. All readers can seek help from game experts for further advice.

Ignoring any of the guidelines or not following the game instructions may lead to getting low scores in the game. Therefore, the author is not responsible for such negligence.

What You Will Find In This Guide?

'Dragon City' is an exciting and addictive game that would keep you engaged for hours. The game rewards your imagination and creativity through its stimulating game play.

From breeding dragons to hatching eggs to building habitats and collecting gems, gold and other valuables, and fighting with rival dragons of your friends to build your magical and floating Dragon City. This game has it all.

You will be provided with a limited number of resources in this game and you are required to utilize them in the best possible manner to build a great Dragon City.

If you are excited to play 'Dragon City' but have no clue about how to grow your city exponentially, you have come to the right place. This beginner's guide includes the best tips, hints, cheats, hacks, and strategy to help you build the greatest and strongest Dragon City.

In short, you get to know everything that will help you become a master of this adventurous and fun packed game. Continue reading and enjoy the highly addictive game known as 'Dragon City'.

So what are you waiting for? Grab your dragons and start building your city!

Chapter 1

Dragon City - An Introduction

Dragon city is an addictive game in which you get to build and decorate your magical and floating dragon city. Engage with opponents all around the world by customizing your dragon team. Train, grow and feed your dragons to make them invincible in combat. Build your city to new heights and become a true Dragon master.

You have the option of breeding and combining up to 10 types of dragons namely flame, nature, metal, terra, ice, electric, sea, pure, legend and dark. Get to experience the best graphics you have seen in a game. There are more than 160 objectives to complete. You can even invite your Facebook friends by sending those gifts.

Sine Dragon City is synced with your Facebook; you can take care of your dragons anytime or anywhere. Embellish your city with farms, decorations, and special buildings. You have the choice of more than 100+ dragons with new dragons added every week. Get to battle with thousands of online dragon teams to earn gems and gold.

The latest version of Dragon City offers new and exclusive dragons for your collection. There are more than 30 new dragons to breed. There are new themed events from all over the world. Premium users can get exclusive offers and get to participate in tournaments at the great stadium.

Chapter 2: Understanding the Basics of the Game

Gold

Gold is the primary currency of the game. It is gained by collecting from your dragons' habitats, selling dragons, dragon eggs, or items, collecting from the dragon market, winning a tournament, or accepting gold gifts from your friends.

Food

Your dragon's experience and level is increased by feeding it food. Dragon food is produced on farms. These farms can be upgraded to produce a variety of plants and better quality produce. Other ways you can obtain food is through the dragon market, on completion of objectives, and buying it with gems. When you produce food, you also gain experience at the cost of gold.

Gems

Gem is the secondary currency of the game but is more valuable than gold. It can be used to buy or trade items. Gems can be obtained by buying them online, by winning battles, by leveling up and by inviting friends to play.

Neighbors

You need neighbors in this game to expand your territory. Here is what your friends need to do in order to become a neighbor.

- Your friends have to be people who have never played Dragon City before.
- Your friends need to accept your request and pass the tutorial.
- Your friends need to accept the messages in the message center.

Game Levels

As you progress through the game and gain experience, you get to unlock more complex features, dragons and buildings. You can gain experience by completing objectives, growing food, clearing obstacles, battling with other dragons and by building things such as habitats and farms. You also get one gem for every level that you clear.

Game Goals

The game provides you with specific objectives to complete at each level. When you have completed an objective, you are rewarded with either gold, experience, gems or food. The list of objectives goes on as you move further in the game. The objectives are related to breeding, hatching, leveling your dragons and building things.

Dragon Book

The dragon book is a collection checklist. You are rewarded for completion of objectives on a per collection basis. Each dragon is counted thrice towards the final tally, once for each stage of Hatching, Juvenile, and Adult. Each collection has 3 to 5 dragons. Depending on your collection, you are rewarded with 2 to 9 gems on completion of each collection. The difficult the collection is, the greater the rewards are.

Chapter 3: Things to Build

Islands

The islands are where you will build your city. Due to the irregular shape and size of islands, you cannot make perfect use of them. Most of the space on the islands will be covered by habitats. You can also acquire building space and expand your city through expansions.

Habitats

Habitats are the place where you keep your dragons. Different types of habitats exist for each element. A dragon can only be placed in a habitat that corresponds to its element. Dragons with more than one element can be placed in either habitat. All basic habitats require a space of 4x4 but legend and pure habitats require a space of 6x6. The following figure will give you a good idea about habitats.

Building Name	Elem	☆	◈ Price	★ XP	🐾	Max ◈	Friends or Building Time
Terra Habitat		1	100	100	2	500	10 seconds
Flame Habitat		2	150	230	2	5,000	10 seconds
Sea Habitat		4	500	500	1	7,500	10 seconds

Nature Habitat		6	1,500	1,500	2	10K	2 mins
Electric Habitat		10	30K	20K	2	12K	4 hours
Ice Habitat		14	75K	50K	1	15K	Instant 3 friends
Metal Habitat		18	100K	100K	2	17K	Instant 4 friends
Dark Habitat		22	500K	250K	2	20K	15 hours
Light Habitat		26	16M	2M	2	40K	12 hours
War Habitat		30	22M	2M 750K	2	60K	18 hours
Pure Habitat		34	30M	3M 750K	2	80K	1 day
Legend Habitat		38	40M	5M	1	350K	1 day 6 hours

Farms

Farms are the most reliable and fastest way to produce food for your dragons and earn experience points. As you move on further in the game, you will be able to upgrade the farms different types of food.

	FARM	LEVEL	COST TO BUILD	XP	SIZE	SELL
	Food Farm	1	100 🍃	100 ⭐	3x3	50 🍃

	Big Food Farm	8	25,000	25,000 ⭐	3x3	12,500
	Huge Food Farm	18	500,000	250,000 ⭐	3x3	250,000

Crystals

Crystals are placed inside a corresponding habitat. For instance, a terra crystal can only be placed inside a terra habitat. Due to their placement inside the habitat, the crystal matching the element of the dragon, even if located in a different habitat, will receive a 20% increase in gold. However, the radius between the crystals and dragons should be of 21 tiles. This will help you earn more gold, as you will be earning gold each minute.

Crystal	Type	Level	Price	XP
		15	250,000	250,000 ⭐
		18	250,000	250,000 ⭐

		21	250,000	250,000 ★
		24	250,000	250,000 ★
		27	250,000	250,000 ★
		30	250,000	250,000 ★
		33	250,000	250,000 ★

| | | 36 | 250,000 | 250,000 |
| | | 39 | 250,000 | 250,000 |

Breeding

In the beginning of the game, you will be taught how to breed your dragon. Next, you will have to select the location such as the Breeding Tree or Breeding Mountain to breed your dragon. There the dragons you select will breed and produce dragon eggs. There are three stages of a dragon's life. At the first stage (level 1), the dragon starts out as a baby, the second stage is the breeding stage (level 4), and in the last they become full-grown dragons (level 7). Feed your dragon to become stronger to fight the battles and produce more gold.

Specials

Specials are irreplaceable buildings that you can only build once throughout the game. However, in order to build some buildings, you will need the help of a friend.

Temples

There are six different types of temples in the game. Each temple helps to level up the dragons and earn money. In addition, each temple has different requirements to obtain it such as the number of friends and the level your dragon is at, but if you have the gold then you can purchase them.

Decorations

Decorations are just there for you to make your islands beautiful and appealing. You can either purchase the decorations from a shop or from a mystery egg gifted to you.

Icon	Tiles	Cost	Level Available	XP
	Stone	100	1	10 ⭐
	Fancy	500	8	10 ⭐

Icon	Plants	Cost	Level Available	XP
	Magic Mushroom	500	1	10 ⭐
	Cat eye Flower	1,000	5	10 ⭐
	Willow Tree	10	10	40 ⭐
	Glowy Flower	5,000	17	10 ⭐

Icon	Flags	Cost	Level Available	XP

	Dragon	250 🪙	1	10 ⭐
	Cloud	2,500 🪙	9	10 ⭐
	Dragon Head	7,500 🪙	16	10 ⭐

Chapter 4: Dragons by Element

1. Terra Dragons

A terra dragon's attacks include earthquake, tumbleweed, and meteor shower. You can train them to learn the sand storm and asteroid attack.

Default attacks

Attack	Element	Base Damage	Duration
Earthquake		550	12 Hours
Meteor Shower		650	12 Hours
Tumble Weed		1050	12 Hours

Trainable attacks

Attack	Element	Base Damage	Duration
Asteroid		1200	24 Hours
Sand Storm		1350	48 Hours

2. Flame Dragons

A flame dragon's attacks include nuclear hit, flame arrows, and lava balls. You can train them to learn the magma storm and flamethrower attack.

Default attacks:

Attack	Element	Base Damage	Duration
Lava Balls	🔥	550	12 Hours
Flaming Arrows	🔥	650	12 Hours
Nuclear Hit	🔥	1050	12 Hours

Trainable attacks:

Attack	Element	Base Damage	Duration
Flamethrower	🔥	1200	24 Hours
Magma Storm	🔥	1350	48 Hours

3. Sea Dragons

A sea dragon's attacks include tsunami, flooding, and storm. You can train them to learn acid rain and whirlpool attack.

Default attacks:

Attack	Element	Base Damage	Duration
Tsunami	🏃	550	12 Hours

Flooding	✳	650	12 Hours
Storm	✳	1050	12 Hours

Trainable attacks:

Attack	Element	Base Damage	Duration
Acid Rain	✳	1200	24 Hours
Whirlpool	✳	1350	48 Hours

4. Nature Dragons

A nature dragon's attacks include punch, poison ivy, stitching roots, and leaf blast. You can train them to learn the rottening spell and beehive attack.

Default attacks:

Attack	Element	Base Damage	Duration
Stitching Roots	🍃	550	12 Hours
Poison Ivy	🍃	650	12 Hours
Leaf Blast	🍃	1050	12 Hours

Trainable attacks:

Attack	Element	Base Damage	Duration
Rottening Spell	🔵	1200	24 Hours
Bee Hive	🔵	1350	48 Hours

5. Electric Dragons

An electric dragon's attacks include laser beam, electric shock, and lightning. You can train them to learn the electro ball and tesla ray attack.

Default attacks:

Attack	Element	Base Damage	Duration
Lightning	⚡	550	12 Hours
Laser Beam	⚡	650	12 Hours
Electric Shock	⚡	1050	12 Hours

Trainable attacks:

Attack	Element	Base Damage	Duration

Electro Ball		1200	24 Hours
Tesla Ray		1350	48 Hours

6. Metal Dragons

A metal dragon's attacks include nail rain, rust, and magneto. You can train them to learn cannon balls and ninja stars attack.

Default attacks:

Attack	Element	Base Damage	Duration
Nail Rain		550	12 Hours
Magneto		650	12 Hours
Rust		1050	12 Hours

Trainable attacks:

Attack	Element	Base Damage	Duration
Cannon Balls		1200	24 Hours
Ninja Stars		1350	48 Hours

7. Ice Dragons

An ice dragon's attacks include frost nova, ice spikes, and snowstorm. You can train them to learn the ice wind and cryogenic freeze attack.

Default attacks:

Attack	Element	Base Damage	Duration
Frost Nova	❄	550	12 Hours
Ice Spikes	❄	650	12 Hours
Snow Storm	❄	1050	12 Hours

Trainable attacks:

Attack	Element	Base Damage	Duration
Icy Wind	❄	1200	24 Hours
Cryogenic Freeze	❄	1350	48 Hours

8. Dark Dragons

A dark dragon's attacks include life drain, ghost cloud, and leech. You can train them to learn the grim reaper and black hole attack.

Default attacks:

Attack	Element	Base Damage	Duration
Life Drain	☾	550	12 Hours

Leech	☾	650	12 Hours
Ghost Cloud	☾	1050	12 Hours

Trainable attacks:

Attack	Element	Base Damage	Duration
The Grim Reaper	☾	1200	24 Hours
Black Hole	☾	1350	48 Hours

9. Light Dragons

A light dragon's attacks include light sword, light star, and light prism. You can train them to learn the enlighting wisdom and out of time attack.

Default attacks:

Attack	Element	Base Damage	Duration
Light Sword	✸	650	48 Hours
Light Prism	✸	750	48 Hours
Light Star	✸	1050	48 Hours

Trainable attacks:

Attack	Element	Base Damage	Duration
Enlightning Wisdom		1200	48 Hours
Out of Time		1350	48 Hours

10. War Dragons

A war dragon's attacks include giant mouth, giant claw, and giant crack. You can train them to learn the war fist and astro hit attack.

Default attacks:

Attack	Element	Base Damage	Duration
Giant Crack		638	48 Hours
Giant Mouth		975	48 Hours
Giant Claw		1050	48 Hours

Trainable attacks:

Attack	Element	Base Damage	Duration
War Fist		1500	48 Hours

Attack	Element	Base Damage	Duration
Astro Hit		1650	48 Hours

11. Pure Dragons

A pure dragon's attacks include pure energy, pure light, and hypnosis. These attacks are trainable as well.

Default and Trainable Attacks:

Attack	Element	Base Damage	Duration
Hypnosis		1500	24 Hours
Pure Energy		1500	48 Hours
Pure Light		1500	48 Hours

12. Legend Dragons

A legendary dragon's attacks include head butting, legendary wind, paralyzing spell, and rainbow attack. You can train them to learn the legend spell and aurora borealis attack.

Default attacks:

Attack	Element	Base Damage	Duration
Legendary Wind		550	12 Hours
Paralyzing Spell		650	12 Hours

Rainbow	∞	1050	12 Hours

Trainable attacks:

Attack	Element	Base Damage	Duration
Aurora Borealis	∞	2100	24 Hours
Legend Spell	∞	2300	48 Hours

Chapter 5: Dragons by Type

Elementals

An elemental dragon that has one element can be bought from the store. In total, there are eleven elements with legend not considered as being one. You can only place an elemental dragon in its own habitat, the Kindergarten, or the Dragonarium. Here is a list informing you the generations that these elemental dragons are placed in:

a) Generation I Elementals: Dark, nature, metal, ice, flame, sea, and electric dragons

b) Generation I-b Elementals: Archangel and War Dragons

c) Generation I-c Elementals: Pure Dragons only

Hybrids

Hybrid dragons have more than one element. This group has the largest number of dragons due to the possibility of breeding two different dragons. The hybrids in this group have only four attacks that they can use in the battlefield. The hybrids have two elements.

The first element is known as the primary and defending element. This element characterizes the type of a dragon the hybrid is. Moreover, this element is used to calculate the damage a hybrid can cause to another opponent during battle. The other element is known as secondary elements and is used to determine the type of attack a hybrid can perform in the battlefield and what other attacks they can learn and train for. You can place the hybrid in a habitat according to their primary and secondary elements. You can breed them with another dragon that possesses either one or both of their elements.

Rare Hybrids

You can get a rare hybrid dragon by breeding a legend dragon with another dragon. In order to breed the rare hybrids, both dragons need to be hybrids. If you do happen to get a rare hybrid, then they can become useful in battles for defeating a legend dragon.

Legends

Since the primary attack of dragons is the most powerful and effective, choose a dragon with primary elements that can be immune to the opponent's primary element with the secondary elements incurring the most damage. Therefore, a legend dragon has no secondary elements, but can only use physical attacks to defeat another dragon. In addition, the legend attack works well in inflicting damage to Legend dragons.

Exclusives

An exclusive dragon is very rare, as they are only introduced when a holiday or event is about to come. You cannot breed them, but an exclusive dragon sold in the store is breedable. Some exclusives can take about 20 hours to hatch. While, there are certain exclusives that require you to be on a certain level to get them. Conversely, an exclusive dragon may require you to have three elements to breed.

Non-Playable

In the game, you will find information about these non-playable dragons and see them in the game, but won't be able to breed or use them. However, some of these dragons can be used for battle, but they are not for keeping. If somehow by hacking or cheating you do obtain the dragon, you can breed them and obtain either a hybrid or an elemental dragon.

Chapter 6: Walkthrough

The Beginning

At the beginning of the game, you are given a dragon to breed. Breeding the two dragons will give you an egg, which will hatch into a baby dragon. If you wish, you can purchase the egg as well. You will have to feed it regularly so it can become strong to win the battles. You will breed the dragons on the Breeding Mountain by selecting "Breed" and then click on the dragon egg to hatch in the Hatchery and wait for the dragon evolution to happen." Once the dragon reaches level seven, it's ready to battle.

Breeding

With the dragons that you have, you will have to experiment breeding two different or same dragons together to see which baby dragon it will produce. You can try the following combination to produce the dragons:

1. Elemental dragon + elemental dragon = unique dragon

2. Elemental + hybrid dragon = not always, but sometimes may produce a new dragon

3. Hybrid + hybrid dragon = not always, but sometimes may produce a new dragon

Getting a new dragon depends on luck and you will have to keep breeding different types of dragons together, which might lead you to obtain a rare dragon.

Cannot Breed

There are some combinations of dragons that cannot be bred. When playing the game, remember that these combinations of dragons cannot be bred:

1. Ice + Fire, Fire + Ice

2. Dark + Water, Water + Dark

3. Electric + Plant, Plant + Electric

4. Electric + Ice, Ice + Electric

5. Dark + Ice, Ice + Dark

Learn to Balance the Resources

There are three types of resources available in the game for you to collect. The resources are gold and food. You can get gold, gems, or experience points by completing quests. You can get food from the Dragon Market and gold from the dragons. Collecting gold is important in this game, as it will help your build farms.

After you have earned a good of amount of gold, immediately start purchasing as many farms as you can, as farms provide food for the dragons. Purchasing many farms will produce more food for your dragons, which will help you level up your dragons faster and generate more gold. On higher levels of the game, the large farms will produce more food for a longer period. However, purchasing the large farms in the beginning will be too expensive.

Selling the Dragons

You should sell your dragons by looking at certain factors. Factors like how much gold do they produce, the level they are at, and the type of dragon it is. After looking at these factors, you can decide on the dragon you want to discard. For instance, look below to see some of the gold earning statistics of dragons at level 7:

1. Water Dragon: 15 gold per minute

2. Earth Dragon: 90 gold per minute

3. Electric Dragon: 60 gold per minute

4. Fire Bird Dragon: 52 gold per minute

5. Fire Dragon: 37 gold per minute

6. Cloud Dragon: 23 gold per minute

7. Star Dragon: 75 gold per minute

8. Spicy Dragon: 45 gold per minute

From breeding, if you get a similar type of dragon you already have, then you can sell it. Another way earning quick money is by breeding your dragons and then selling them for money. Furthermore, breeding rare dragons together will earn you more money. Still, you should only sell your dragons when you need money the most, as having dragons earn you more money than selling them.

Also, remember that the level your dragon is at when selling doesn't matter. You will still earn the same amount of gold if you were selling it at a lower level. The only difference in the selling price is that the value of each dragon differs depending on the type of dragon it is. Look below to get an idea of how each dragon's value differs according to their type:

1. Earth Dragon: 50 gold

2. Volcano Dragon: 1000 gold

3. Laser: 50000 gold

4. Ice Dragon: 375 gold

5. Tropical Dragon: 300 gold

6. Waterfall Dragon: 5000 gold

7. Electric Dragon: 150 gold

Dragon Battle

In order to start battling other players' dragons, you need to build a stadium. At one time, only three dragons are allowed to fight. Players can have two or three dragons fighting for them. Each player then takes turns striking each other's dragons. The winner is announced when all the dragons of the opponent are defeated. Here are some general rules to remember about battling dragons:

1. Switching dragons during battle, counts as a turn.

2. You can battle in the tournament once every 12 hours.

3. You can unlock stronger attacks by leveling up your dragons.

4. After battling in the stadium, you want an additional challenge then you can click on the globe icon to enter the combat world to battle against other players from around the world.

5. In the combat world, you can compete against other players three times a day every six hours.

6. If you get defeated in the combat world, you will not lose your dragons.

The element of the attack and the element of the dragon you are fighting determine an attack's effectiveness and strength. Opposing elements such as fire will have a much stronger and damaging attack when attacking an ice element. The below list explains the four types of attack and their damaging ratio:

1. Critical Attack: 2X the damage

2. Normal Attack: 1X the damage

3. Weak Attack: 1/2X the damage

4. No Attack: 0X the damage

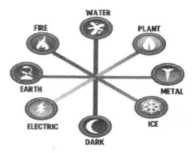

This chart determines how much damage an element

The first elements of the hybrid dragon will determine the dragon's weaknesses and strengths. For instance, if you are fighting a hybrid dragon, then check the first element of the dragon such as earth or fire. If the first element is fire, the weaknesses will be water or electric.

The chart below tells how much damage an element can occur on the other element.

	DEFENDER							
ATTACKER	Earth	Fire	Water	Plant	Electric	Ice	Metal	Dark
Earth	0x	1x	0x	2x	1x	1x	0x	1x
Fire	0x	0x	2x	1x	1x	2x	0x	1x
Water	1x	2x	0x	1x	2x	0x	1x	1x
Plant	1x	0x	0x	1x	2x	1x	1x	2x
Electric	0x	2x	2x	1x	1x	1x	2x	1x
Ice	2x	0x	1x	2x	1x	1x	1x	0x
Metal	2x	0x	1x	1x	0x	2x	1x	1x
Dark	1x	1x	2x	1x	1x	1x	1x	1x

Chapter 7: Tips, Strategies & Cheats

Guide to Farming: Collecting Food

Farming is an important aspect of the game. You need to feed your dragons so they can get stronger to fight in battles, level up faster, and produce more gold. Read below to find out the types of farms available to build and what food you should grow:

a) Food Farm

You get this farm at level 1. This farm produces 100 gold and earns you 100 experience points.

b) Big Food Farm

You get this farm when you reach level 8. This farm cost 25,000 gold to build and you can gain 25,000 experience points.

c) Huge Food Farm

You get this farm when you reach level 18. From this farm you can earn 500,000 gold and gain 250,000 experience points.

What Food to Grow

You should grow food according to the time you spend away from the game. For instance, if you plan to sleep and check the game tomorrow, grow crops that take a long time to grow. If it's the other way around and you playing immediately, grow crops that take a short time to grow. Below is a list of crops and their information so choose wisely:

1. Food Farm Food

Hot Dragon Chili

It takes five minutes to grow and you can purchase it for 250 gold. This crop will give you 50 food and 250 experience points.

Dragon Bell

It takes 30 minutes to grow and costs 50 gold. It will give you 10 food and 25 experience points.

Caterpillar Lily

It takes 30 minutes to grow and will cost you 1,000 gold. It will provide you 150 food and with 1,000 experience points.

2. Big Food Farm

Unicorn Horn
This crop takes two hours to grow, costs 5000 gold, will give you 400 food, and 5,000 experience points.

Ladybird Blossom
This food takes six hours to grow, costs 15,000 gold, will give you 1,000 food, and 15,000 experience points.

Rainbow Flower
This crop takes 12 hours to grow, costs 75,000 gold, will give you 3,000 food, and 75,000 experience points.

3. Huge Food Farm

Spike Balls
This crop takes 24 hours to grow, it will cost you 50,000 gold, will give you 10,000 food, and 250,000 experience points.

Flesh Eaters
This crop takes 36 hours to grow, costs 1 million gold, gives you 20,000 food, and 500,000 experience points.

Star Shines
This crop takes 48 hours to grow, costs 5 million gold, will give you 100,000 food, and 2,500,000 experience points.

*Tip: It is recommended that you choose the crops based on how much gold you have. If you can be patient, then the quick crops are your best bet. However, if you are planning to go on a long vacation and know you will be away from the game for a few days, pick the crops that take longer to grow.

Gem Guide: Getting More Gems

Follow these steps to gain more gems:

1. Participate in the Combat World to get two gems and gold each time you fight. Every 6 hours, you can combat three players.
2. Construct a stadium for your dragons to fight in and earn two gems and gold.
3. From the daily bonus reward, you can win 45 gems.
4. Each time you level up as a player, you will be rewarded with one gem.
5. Every Monday a reward is handed out that rewards you with four gems if you select the correct prize.
6. Each time you log in to the game, gems will be awarded to you at the end of the day. The more you log in, the higher the chance of getting more gems.

Tip: There are sites available online that provide players with a hacking software, which lets them hack the game and obtain gold, gems, and food. For legal reasons, we can't tell you which sites to use, but a quick Google search will show you the sites you need.

Gold Guide: Getting More Gold

Dragons residing in their habitat produce gold for you. Different dragons have different speed of producing gold. The speed of producing gold will increase as your dragons level up. Conversely, a habitat has their own restrictions in how much gold they can hold at one time. If you neglect to collect the gold and the habitat gets full, then the dragons in it will stop producing gold. Follow these strategies to get more gold:

1. The Legendary dragon has a high gold producing rate and their habitat can hold plenty of gold.
2. If you don't have a Legendary dragon yet, then invest on building earth habitats. Boost the earth habitats by using earth boost and make sure that the dragons living in it are at level 10. Place the earth boost in a location where all the earth habitats can benefit from. In doing so, the production of gold will increase.

*Tip: Build five to six earth habitats and get four earth boosts, as it will help boost the production of gold by eighty percent. Keep in mind that you would have to continually collect gold from the earth habitats since they can't hold a lot of gold.

3. Instead of building an Earth habitat, you can build a Dark habitat and use a Hedgehog dragon. Unlike Earth habitats, Dark habitats can hold a lot more gold and the Hedgehog dragon produce gold at a much faster rate. For this strategy, you can use two separate boosts, one Earth boost, and one dark boost. Your gold production will increase by 160%.

*Tip: Although this strategy is more effective than the previous one, this strategy is more difficult to do. It's difficult to do because a Hedgehog dragon is difficult to breed. It can take hours for the dragon to hatch and breed. In addition, you may get a Venom dragon, instead of a Hedgehog dragon.

Level Guide: Leveling Up Fast

There are various ways that you can as player level up fast in the gamer. Listed below are some strategies that you can use to level up fast:

1. You can build a farm and later sell it to build another farm. Each time you build a farm, you will earn more experience points. The farm that gives you the most experience is the largest farm available in the game, but it is very costly. Therefore, the wise choice is to build a big farm because it affordable and gives you good experience. Building a farm to gain more experience is the quickest technique to get more experience, as unlike other buildings it doesn't have a building time.

2. Another way to gain experience and level up fast is to use "boost" instead of building a farm. Although boost is very expensive and has a long building time, it gives you plenty of experience points.

3. Building large habitats to host your dragons in can provide you with numerous experience points. However, this approach is costly and inconvenient.

4. For experience points, you can grow plenty of food. Growing lots of food will benefit your dragons' level up faster as well as you. In order for you to grow food, you need gold.

Fighting Guide: Winning Combinations

1. Metal Element

Weak Against: Electric

Resistances: Metal, Earth, and Fire

Strong Against: Earth and Ice

Opposed by: Fire and Electric

2. Ice Element

Weak Against: Metal and Fire

Resistances: Water

Strong Against: Earth

Opposed by: Fire

3. Earth Element

Weak Against: Metal, Water, and Ice

Resistances: Fire and Ice

Strong Against: None

Opposed by: Water and Metal

4. Water Element

Weak Against: Dark and Fire

Resistances: Plant, Water, and Earth

Strong Against: Electric, Fire, and Earth

Opposed by: Ice

5. Fire Element

Weak Against: Electric and Water

Resistances: Plant, Fire, Metal, and Ice

Strong Against: Plant, Water, and Ice

Opposed by: Fire, Metal, and Earth

6. Plant Element

Weak Against: Ice and Earth

Resistances: Dark

Strong Against: Water

Opposed by: Fire

7. Electric Element

Weak Against: Water

Resistances: Metal and Electric

Strong Against: Metal, Water, and Fire

Opposed by: Earth

8. Legendary

Weak Against: None

Resistances: Natural Attacks

9. Dark Element

Weak Against: Fire and Electric

Resistances: Earth and Ice

Breeding Guide: Hybrid Combinations

Earth Dragon Hybrids

Earth + Fire= Flaming Rock Dragon or Volcano Dragon

Earth + Plant= Tropical Dragon, Mud Dragon, Cactus Dragon, or Waterfall Dragon

Earth + Electric= Chameleon Dragon or Star Dragon

Earth + Ice= Snow Flake Dragon or Alpine Dragon

Earth + Metal= Armadillo Dragons

Earth + Dark= Venom Dragon or Hedgehog Dragon

Fire Dragon Hybrids

Fire + Earth= Flaming Rock Dragon or Volcano Dragon

Fire+ Water= Blizzard Dragon or Cloud Dragon

Fire + Plant= Spicy Dragon or Firebird Dragon

Fire + Electric= Laser Dragon or Hot Metal Dragon

Fire + Metal= Medieval Dragon or Steam punk Dragon

Fire + Dark= Vampire Dragon or Dark Fire Dragon

Water Dragon Hybrids

Water + Earth = Mud Dragon

Water + Fire = Cloud Dragon or Blizzard Dragon

Water + Plant = Nenufar Dragon

Water + Plant = Coral Dragon

Water + Electric = Lantern Fish Dragon or Storm Dragon

Water + Ice = Ice cube Dragon or Ice Cream Dragon

Water + Metal = Mercury Dragon or Seashell Dragon

Plant Dragon Hybrids

Plant + Earth = Tropical Dragon

Plant + Fire = Firebird Dragon or Spicy Dragons

Plant + Water = Nenufar Dragon or Coral Dragon

Plant + Ice = Dandelion Dragon or Mojito Dragon

Plant + Metal = Jade Dragon or Dragonfly Dragon

Plant + Dark = Carnivore Plant Dragon or Rattlesnake Dragon

Electric Dragon Hybrids

Electric + Earth = Star Dragon or Chameleon Dragon

Electric + Fire = Laser Dragon

Electric + Fire = Hot Metal Dragon

Electric + Water = Lantern Fish Dragon or Storm Dragon

Electric + Metal = Golden Dragon or Battery Dragon

Electric + Dark = Neon Dragon

Electric + Ice = Moose Dragon

Ice Dragon Hybrids

Ice + Earth = Alpine Dragon or Snow Flake Dragon

Ice + Water = Ice cube Dragon or Ice Cream Dragon

Ice + Plant = Dandelion Dragon or Mojito Dragon

Ice + Metal = Platinum Dragon

Ice + Electric = Moose Dragon

Metal Dragon Hybrids

Metal + Fire = Medieval Dragon or Steam punk Dragon

Metal + Water = Mercury Dragon or Seashell Dragon

Metal + Ice = Platinum Dragon

Metal + Plant = Jade Dragon or Dragonfly Dragon

Metal + Electric = Golden Dragon or Battery Dragon

Metal + Dark = Zombie Dragon

Dark Dragon Hybrids

Dark + Earth = Hedgehog Dragon or Venom Dragon

Dark + Fire = Vampire Dragon or Dark Fire Dragon

Dark + Plant = Carnivore Plant Dragon or Rattlesnake Dragon

Dark + Electric = Neon Dragon

Dark + Ice = Penguin Dragon

Dark + Metal = Zombie Dragon

Hybrid Rare Dragons

(Created after breeding the dragon hybrids mentioned above together)

Dark + Mud = Poo Dragon

Medieval + Alpine, Laser + Dandelion, or Firebird+ Ice= Cool Fire Dragon

Medieval + Alpine = Soccer Dragon, Pearl Dragon, or Flaming Rock Dragon

Medieval + Alpine, Pearl + Alpine, Jade + Star, Zombie + Mud, or Pearl + Flaming Rock= Armadillo Dragon

Neon + Nenufar, Rattlesnake + Lantern fish, or Neon + Cloud Dragons= Pirate Dragon

Zombie + Mud = Petroleum Dragon

Laser + Dandelion, Firebird + Fluorescent, Firebird + Star, Jade + Star, or Neon + Nenufar= Gummy Dragon

Laser + Dandelion= Fluorescent Dragon

Cool fire + Gummy= Laser

Legendary Hybrid Dragons

Legendary hybrid dragons are the most difficult to produce. If you are lucky, you might get a legendary hybrid dragon. If not, then you will have to keep trying until you get one. These combinations given below just serve as a guide to let you what combinations are the most successful in obtaining a legendary hybrid dragon:

Cool Fire + Soccer = Legendary Dragon or Crystal Dragon

Gummy + Cool Fire = Mirror Dragon

Gummy + Cool Fire or Soccer + Cool Fire= Wind Dragon

Tip: By breeding Medieval Dragons and Alpine dragons, you will get a higher chance of getting different types of hybrids.

Breeding Guide: Pure Dragon Combinations

In order to create a pure hybrid, you need to have a legendary hybrid first. You can produce a pure dragon by breeding any two legendary hybrids together, which are Crystal, Mirror, Wind, and Legendary. If you do get a pure dragon, then you can use it to make other pure dragons. Try the following combinations to make a pure dragon:

Pure + Plant = Pure Plant Dragon

Pure + Fire = Pure Fire Dragon

Pure + Earth = Pure Earth Dragon

Pure + Water = Pure Water Dragon

Pure + Electric = Pure Electric Dragon

Pure + Ice = Pure Ice Dragon

Pure + Metal = Pure Metal Dragon

Pure + Dark = Pure Dark Dragon

It will take 48 hours to breed a pure dragon with another 48 hours to hatch them. Therefore, you won't be able to breed other dragons. So, prior to breeding your pure dragons make sure your other dragons are battle ready.

Enter the Dragon City

Dragon City is an entertaining, fun, and challenging game. It's a game, which has captivated many players from around the world. Dragon city keeps people fascinated by introducing new breeds of dragons. There are over a 50 types of dragons available for people to try their luck at getting. Dragon City has no age limit and people of all ages are addicted to it. The features the game offer is the most impressive part of this game.

From the awesome battles, dragons, gold, gems, food, buildings, and farms have made Dragon City the most played game. You can play other players from around the world who share your enthusiasm for the game. Once you start playing the game, you won't be able to put it down. With the help of this guide, download and play the game.

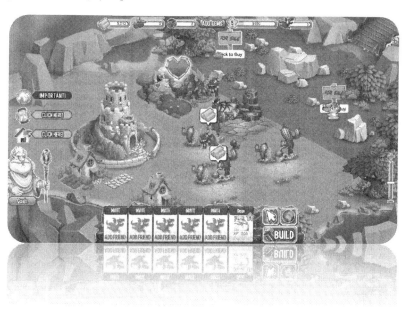

Maple Tree Books

If you want to get access to upcoming books on various topics, 'like' our Facebook page to be informed. We always offer the books for free for 5 days when they are first released. You can download them when they are free and benefit from them :)

Go to this website and enter your name and email to join our mailing list.

https://www.Facebook.com/mapletreebooks

And oh, dont forget to leave a review :)

Even if you did not benefit from this book at all, we still want to hear from your feedback so we can improve in the future :)

Alternatively you can join our mailing list

http://www.MapleTreeBooks.com

You can join our Twitter page as well

https://Twitter.com/MapleTreeBooks1

Thanks for reading :)

We wish you success in this life and in the next.

Made in the USA
San Bernardino, CA
22 July 2019